Fifty Ways
to Lead
and Love It!

Cheryl Cran

Note for Librarians: a cataloguing record for this book that includes Dewey Decimal Classification and US Library of Congress numbers is available from the Library and Archives of Canada. The complete cataloguing record can be obtained from their online database at:

www.collectionscanada.ca/amicus/index-e.html

ISBN 1-4120-0928-6

Printed in Victoria, BC, Canada

To request permission to reproduce any part of this book, or to engage Cheryl Cran for your next conference or in-house event, please contact:

Synthesis at Work - Suite 1000, 355 Burrard St. Vancouver, B.C. V6C 2G8, CANADA

Toll-free: 1-877-900-5010

Facsimile: 604-552-8588

E-mail: *info@cherylcran.com*

Web site: *www.cherylcran.com*

Cover design by Christina Szokendi, Pivotal Concepts

Editorial and production services by GF Murray Creative Information Solutions

TRAFFORD

Offices in Canada, USA, Ireland, UK and Spain

Book sales for North America and international:
Trafford Publishing, 6E–2333 Government St.,
Victoria, BC v8t 4p4 CANADA
phone 250 383 6864 (toll-free 1 888 232 4444) • fax 250 383 6804; email to orders@trafford.com
Book sales in Europe:
Trafford Publishing (uk) Ltd., Enterprise House, Wistaston Road Business Centre,
Wistaston Road, Crewe, Cheshire cw2 7rp UNITED KINGDOM
phone 01270 251 396 (local rate 0845 230 9601)
facsimile 01270 254 983; orders.uk@trafford.com

10 9 8 7 6 5 4 3 2

Fifty Ways to Lead and Love It!

Foreword

by Sam Horn, author of *Tongue Fu!*®, *What's Holding You Back?*, *ConZentrate*, and *Take The Bully By The Horns*

There are many books on leadership to choose from, so you may be wondering, "Why should I read this one?"

Simply put, Cheryl's approach to managing people is unique. She knows, from many years of first-hand experience and from working with individuals and organizations around the world, that there is no *one* right way to lead—there are *many* right ways to lead. The management style we choose to use ought to be based on the circumstances, the tenure of the employees, and the goals of that particular group and situation.

That's why this book provides a variety of ways to motivate, guide, and manage your team.

You'll find this easy to read and full of real-life suggestions you'll want to put into practice immediately. You'll also find yourself enjoying success stories from people just like yourself who have already used these ideas to produce bottom-line results. You might want to keep this book on your desk as a handy reference for those almost-daily conflicts and challenges that are part of supervising people with different personalities and needs.

For instance, item # 9, "Hold 'Em... Accountable" could be useful if you're frustrated with an employee who has been shirking responsibility for his or her work duties. Item # 2, "What's Your Brand?" can help you determine if the image you are projecting as a professional is aligned with how you want and need to be perceived within your organization and industry.

Consider this book your "pocket coach." There's no need to go it alone as long as you have the wise, insightful advice contained in this handy reference. Read it and reap.

First Words

Leadership often gets a bum rap.

Some leaders might say:

"I feel like a glorified babysitter!"

"They don't care as much as I do."

"They just don't get it."

Well, all of the above comments are true. At times leaders do feel like nothing more than glorified babysitters. It's also true that most employees won't necessarily care as much as the owner, CEO or CFO of a company does. And sometimes our managers and employees *don't* get it.

Even with these expressed frustrations those of us in leadership choose to stay in it because most of the time it's *fun*!

Yes, fun, rewarding and satisfying.

Cynics will not enjoy this book. If you are frustrated much of the time with the challenges of leadership you may want to re-evaluate your career choice. The best way to lead is with full engagement, a desire to learn, a keen interest in growth and a fire in your belly for results and fun.

If you're not having fun anymore or it's never been fun, it's time to take a long look at why. Ask yourself some questions.

- What were your expectations of your leadership role in the first place?
- Did you have the training and preparation you felt you needed before stepping into the role?
- Did you fully communicate your expectations to your people, your boss and your clients?
- Are you willing to acknowledge that some of your frustrations have been self-created?
- Could you be suffering from burnout?
- When is the last time you attended a management class? Went on a management retreat? Or took some allotted time to focus on your vision, goals and direction?

Powerful leaders (and by powerful I mean centred and influential ones who possess a strong ability to motivate others to high performance) have an optimistic outlook and pragmatic approach to solutions. As soon as cynicism or negativity creeps into our attitudes and behaviours we need to look at why.

It's likely that you are already doing at least forty of the fifty items in this book. You may have more strength in and mastery over some areas than others.

I don't profess to provide earth-shaking new management information. If you take three or four ideas away and then put into action one of them—from any book or seminar—then you have made a worthwhile investment.

Consider this book as a perspective on leadership that you may not have considered, or for that matter, that you may have considered but never actually put into practice. Let this book be a reminder of what you know needs to be done!

Cheryl

Leader, Know Thyself

People travel to wonder at the height of mountains, at the huge waves of the sea, at the long courses of rivers, at the vast compass of the ocean, at the circular motion of the stars, and pass themselves without wondering.

St Augustine

The greatest leaders of corporations, associations, non-profit groups and volunteer boards are able to guide others to achieve incredible things. In my experience as a consultant working with CEOs and management teams, the trait unique to their success is the ability to see themselves as they are.

The leaders that others want to follow have a highly-developed ability to self-lead. Their sharp awareness of the extent of their contribution to the team dynamic as well as their honest self-assessment of their overall skill set allows them to lead with integrity. They are able to inspire high levels of trust.

The most admired leaders are those who are completely honest with themselves about their strengths and weaknesses. Auto industry executive Lee Iacocca was very aware of his strengths and weaknesses. He was quoted as saying, "I don't need to know how to put a car together. I do need to know how to motivate those who put those cars together and to give them a vision."

Action

- Draw a line down the middle of a piece of paper. On the left side make a list of your strengths and on the right side make a list of traits you could improve.
- Set goals to build your skills in areas for improvement.
- Make your team aware that you are actively working on improving certain skill sets.

Allow others to challenge your identity. What is the gap between how they see you and how you see yourself? Everyone's perspective is their reality; you may think you are strong in a certain area of leadership while your employees may think you could work on your communication style.

Strong leaders are open to change and growth and willingly welcome the challenge to examine their abilities.

Why You'll Love It

The more aware you are of what you need to improve, the better equipped you are to match perceptions to action. This lets you build deeper relationships with your employees and clients.

Why They'll Love It

As you demonstrate your willingness to self-examine and to actively work on improving, you inspire your team to do the same. This motivates them to higher levels of engagement with your leadership and direction.

What's Your Brand?

The more you like yourself the less you are like anyone else. This is what makes you unique.

Walt Disney

You may know who you are and what you stand for, but does everyone else?

In Tom Peters' book *The Brand You 50* (Knopf, 1999) he makes a strong case that every person is a brand. Who people are and how they project who they are can make powerful impressions on peers, employees and clients. Corporations understand the power of a corporate brand, but remember that corporations consist of people and each person is his or her own brand.

Think of a famous leader like Rudy Giuliani. What one

word would you use to describe him? If you said "courage" you would be among the 90 percent of people who were asked this question and answered the same way. Giuliani's brand is "courage".

Think of other leaders within your organization—what one word would you use to describe each of them? That one word, for good or bad, is the "brand" they have developed by their words, actions and results.

Action

- What is one word that you would use to describe yourself as a leader?
- Ask your employees or team members to describe your leadership with one word.
- Make a list of five things you stand for.

When employees and co-workers know you and your brand as a leader, and you communicate your brand consistently, you have given them parameters with which to operate around you. When speaking in front of a group I will often say, "Here's what you can expect from me, in one word. I am efficient: I talk fast, move fast, I like to have fun and get results. Let's get started."

The response is always positive. Often people come up to

6 me at the end of the presentation thanking me for letting them know my style. It allows them to adapt and warm up to me more quickly, and they can more easily establish how we are going to move forward together.

Why You'll Love It

Your awareness of your personal brand becomes your starting point from which all words and behaviours stem. You will be more focused when you behave in alignment with your self-identified brand.

Why They'll Love It

When others understand your brand they know what you stand for and what they can expect from you. This in turn allows them to make decisions that align with your brand of leadership.

Tell 'Em
What to Expect

A manager's personal style—how good he or she is at exchanging information—contributes more to a department's efficiency than the results of any structured or organizational brilliance.

Mark H McCormack

I was promoted to my first management role at the age of twenty-three and had nine people report to me. Let's just say that the first few months were hell, partly because I was promoted with zero training in how to manage other people. I could perform at high levels on my own but I had a difficult time transferring that ability to leading others. Management training gave me skills and tools that eased the leadership challenges I had been facing, such as working with employees who were all older than me, and the aggressive leadership style I had adopted in an effort to earn their respect.

When I came back I communicated the new ground rules. They were:

1. If you have a problem with me, come to me directly.
2. If we can't resolve the issue we will invite my boss in to discuss it among the three of us.
3. If you have a problem with a co-worker go to them directly first.
4. If you are uncomfortable approaching the co-worker, come to me and we will have a three-way conversation to resolve the issue.
5. Before you come to me with a general problem please be prepared to present three possible solutions.

Once the parameters of how we would work together were clearly communicated, I put my expectations in writing and posted them on the wall in my office. I found my employees becoming much more proactive about seeking their own solutions.

When employees complained, or did not bring solutions to the table, I would simply turn to look at the list. They would smile and would often say, "I'll come back once I have given this more thought." It was a win-win for everyone.

Over time they began to come to me with solutions and there was less conflict among co-workers and in the team overall. These expectations also kept me from being frustrated with conflicts taken over my head, as my employees now knew to come to me first. In the next six months our team grew to be number one in productivity and sales results in the district.

The world is longing for leaders with conviction, direction and passion—let everyone know what you will not tolerate and what you celebrate. Communicate what they can expect from you verbally and in writing.

Action

- Using the examples I have given, create your own list of the expectations you have for your team.
- Post the list in your office and give a copy to each employee.
- Announce the expectations at a team meeting.

Why You'll Love It

Once you have thought out and clearly communicated your expectations you will find yourself feeling less like a glorified babysitter and more like a leader enjoying the rewards of team responsiveness.

Why They'll Love It

When the team understands your expectations they have rules to play by. It is easier to be creative and autonomous within known parameters.

When You "Assume"

To get others to do what you want them to do, you must see things through their eyes.

David J Schwartz

Assumptions are one of the major causes of relationship trouble. As leaders our success is based on our ability to manage and build relationships. We can get frustrated and irritated by the results of assumptions like:

My team knows how to do this particular task.

They will do it the same way I do.

They will care as much as I do.

They will work as hard as I do.

You get the point. These are all assumptions based on how we see the world.

Communicating expectations in a group meeting and in writing are important opportunities to minimize assumptions within your team as a whole. You also need to communicate what you expect from each person on your team individually.

Clearly define what each employee needs to do his or her job at the highest level. Present those expectations in writing, and in regular one-on-one coaching meetings address where the employee needs to further develop his or her skills.

Action

- Ask yourself the following questions:
    What do I assume my employees should know?
    Do they honestly know it?
    Have I provided opportunities for my employees to learn what they need to know?
- Review job descriptions.
    Are they current?
    In what areas does the employee need further development or training?
- List five things you expect from each person in his or her job.
- With the employee, list actions he or she will take to meet those expectations.

- Follow up on a consistent basis and praise the employee
  when there is progress.

Why You'll Love It

When you take the time to really think about your assumptions of how others "should" behave or what they "should" know you find out what needs to be clarified. This diminishes your frustration and allows you to be more patient and tolerant of others' working styles.

Why They'll Love It

When you give employees the opportunity to learn how to perform at the highest possible level they feel valued, and gain a stronger commitment to doing the job to your high expectations.

Get It Done Right: Delegate!

Keep in mind the better you understand what you want and why you want it, the better your chances will be of acquiring it.

Fred Jandt

Great leaders appreciate the merits of delegation. They have stopped believing the common rationalizations that cause many of us to resist it in the first place. Some of those include:

- I can do it faster and better, and I'll know when it's done.
- It takes too long to teach someone else to do it.
- What if they mess up?
- What if I forget that I delegated it?
- My employees are already very busy as it is.

These are all common traps that keep us from learning the fine art of delegation. As an entrepreneur I have had to learn to delegate out of necessity. Think about your role as a leader: is your time spent doing things that your employees could be doing? Would you be a stronger leader if you could lighten the load of tasks you have become comfortable doing, and instead focus your time on planning, goal-setting and coaching?

If we buy into the reasons why we can't delegate, we are contributing to a self-defeating pattern that will never change. You have probably heard the saying by Anonymous (who, by the way, always has the best sayings): "If you want to get what you have always gotten, just keep doing what you have always done."

The art of delegating is a learned skill. Leaders who have become masters at delegating have invested the time to teach others how to do a task or project properly and have followed up, coached and encouraged. This investment of time at the outset is recouped many times over in increased personal productivity on your part and in the long run overall.

Avoiding the non-delegation trap is actually easier than it appears. Getting the job done right the first time by the employee means we need to delegate succinctly and with clearly-outlined expectations.

The rules of successful delegation are:

1. Tell them.
2. Have them tell you.
3. Write it down.
4. Have them write it down.
5. Show them.
6. Have them show you.

Leaders who delegate in this way enjoy a 95 percent success rate for having the task or project completed within their expectations.

Action

- Make a list of ten things you currently do on a regular basis that could be delegated.
- Identify who would be best suited for each item on the list.
- Set aside an hour a week to train each person on how to perform the delegated tasks or projects.
- Make a note of the items you have delegated, and ask the employee to keep track also. Follow up at the halfway point and then just before the task or project is due.
- Set a goal to delegate one task or project per week to a member of your team so that all items on your list are delegated within a ten-week period.

Why You'll Love It

When you learn to use the art of delegation your stress levels decrease significantly and your ability to focus on higher-level tasks and projects increases.

Why They'll Love It

The benefits to employees include:

- Increased respect in you as a leader as you trust them to take on new tasks or projects,
- Increased job satisfaction, because you have given them opportunities to learn and grow, and
- The chance to show skills and strengths that may not have been previously evident.

Don't Fence Them In

The ultimate responsibility of a leader is to facilitate other people's development as well as his or her own.

Fred Pryor

When I conducted a survey recently I discovered that many employees are frustrated with their bosses' lack of willingness to put them in another role or to give them a chance to show their talents in specific projects.

Leaders can be guilty of limited awareness of the capabilities of employees. Employees who have regular and ongoing coaching sessions with their bosses typically have higher levels of satisfaction and are able to communicate their desire to take on more responsibility or projects that will showcase their abilities.

One of the major causes of low morale within a team is boredom. People are looking for excitement, challenge and change, and it is our responsibility as leaders to provide every opportunity for them to get it.

Action

- Meet with your employees to update goals and cross-training opportunities every ninety days.
- Take a risk—let someone do a project that is outside his or her job scope but that would challenge the employee (but don't set him or her up for failure!)
- When assigning new projects, make employees fully accountable. Set them up for success by providing all of the details they need to complete the task or project at the highest possible level. Make them the CEO of the project and let them succeed.
- Change things around! Mix it up! Be aware of your own comfort zone and your resistance to having someone new take on a job or project.

Why You'll Love It

You will enjoy greater creativity from your team and a renewed willingness to take on new tasks.

Why They'll Love It

Employees who are set up to succeed perform at higher levels, have greater respect for their leaders, and are more willing to volunteer for other tasks and projects.

Split Personalities are Good

Whenever two people meet there are really six people present. There is each man as he sees himself, each man as the other person sees him, and each man as he really is.

William James

Intuitively you have probably adjusted to each individual on your team over time. But what if you knew the two main personality or communication styles of each person you interact with in a day? More important, what if you knew the strategies that would guarantee success when communicating with them?

I'm sure you have heard of Myers-Briggs and other personality profiles as invaluable tools for understanding not only your own personal style but the personality styles of others

22   as well. In my first book *Say What You Mean, Mean What You Say* I present four "D" quadrants as a tool to identify specific personality styles and then provide tips on how to get successful results with each style. Once we understand that people aren't purposely trying to tick us off and we begin to communicate in a way that matches their personality styles we decrease conflict and increase effectiveness in our relationships.

Profile each of your employees, not just yourself. When I facilitate team training sessions, we do a personality profile exercise to quickly see what makes each team member behave the way they do based on personality. It also helps participants understand that other team members aren't purposely trying to annoy them. This is one way to build tolerance within a team.

Everyone's personality incorporates all four styles but people usually communicate from their two predominant styles. It is one thing to know your own style but it's very powerful when you can quickly recognize another person's style and adapt to it. This facilitates quick understanding and generates solutions much quicker too!

Dictator/Driver	Dancer
Moves and talks quickly	Moves and talks quickly
Likes fast solutions	Big-picture focus
Results oriented	Hates details
Driven to succeed	Likes to have fun
Large ego	Loves people
Time conscious	Likes change
Little patience	Great at starting, not at finishing
Can be abrupt	May appear too pie-in-the-sky

Detailer	Deflector
Measured movements/speech	Moves and talks carefully
Analytical	Needs to be liked
Wants proof, charts and graphs	Risk-averse
Prefers things in writing	Takes longer to express ideas
Hates public displays of emotion	Dislikes power plays
Can be a perfectionist	Cares about others
	Can be overly sensitive

Action

- Hold a team session or hire a consultant to conduct a personality profile meeting for you and your team.

- Share all the results with everybody—make them visible and accessible, so team members can understand how to interact successfully with each other.
- Review personality styles regularly to keep everyone aware of differences in values, work habits and behaviours.

Why You'll Love It

By identifying the personality and communication styles of all team players you show a willingness to respect differences within the team and to adapt to their individual styles. You will save time by knowing how to approach each person for greater success and results.

Why They'll Love It

Employees learn to work with opposing personality and communication styles, which builds their ability to handle conflict and to tolerate differences among team members.

Use Conflict as an Opportunity

The way I see it, if you want the rainbow, you gotta put up with the rain.

Dolly Parton

Courageous leaders understand that conflict is not to be avoided; rather, it can build greater understanding and spark creative solutions. Some leaders get caught in the "triangle trap" when dealing with conflict, so it is important to recognize what the trap is and how to stay out of it. When a leader gets involved in employee conflicts before allowing the two individuals involved to work it out first, that's the triangle trap. A scenario may look like this:

1. Employee #1 comes to the leader and complains about employee #2.

2. The leader says, "Let me talk to employee #2."
3. Employee #1 feels good because he or she tattled and the boss is going to fix it.
4. The leader calls in employee #2 and says, "Employee #1 has a problem with you."
5. Employee #1 gets defensive and may retaliate by behaving even more negatively. The relationship between the two employees erodes even further.

When we as leaders step in to make things better we are falling into the trap of taking on employees' responsibility to work out issues in a constructive way. We are obliged to provide the training and skills that allow our employees to handle conflict appropriately.

What would be the preferred outcome of the scenario above? The leader asks employee #1 if he or she has talked to employee #2. If the employee says no, we provide gentle coaching on how to approach the other person, and provide support and feedback once they have gone to the other employee. If the employee doesn't feel comfortable with that, then we can offer to facilitate a conversation with a focus on creating a solution and maintaining mutual accountability.

By teaching our people how to confront conflict

constructively and manage it, we are building strong leadership abilities in our employees and providing an environment where conflict leads to creative solutions.

Action

- Hold a team meeting with the sole purpose of coming up with a process for handling disagreements or differences of opinion about a process or project.
- Break your team into two or three groups with flip charts. Ask them to brainstorm a code of conduct for each team player, to be used in future conflicts. Then bring the results of each group forward to the larger group to establish a common code of conduct for everyone.
- Ask them what conflicts they have experienced or could potentially experience within the team. Have them agree on a process for handling each situation.
- Have them write down five steps to resolution whenever two or more of the team cannot agree.
- Once the resolution process is agreed upon print the steps out in large type, laminate them and post them in every team member's work area.

Don't assume that the skills to manage conflict are

inherent to your team. In most cases the majority of people do one of three things with conflict: they either avoid it, or they confront it negatively or inappropriately. Conflict resolution needs to be taught, and a structure such as a five-step process for managing disagreements can set ground rules for moving forward when faced with conflict.

Why You'll Love It

You will feel greater satisfaction with your team's ability to self-manage conflict and you will also notice greater creativity in the solutions the team comes up with.

Why They'll Love It

Team members will feel more confident in speaking their minds and in having open conversations with other team members. They will increase their productivity because conflict resolution will occur more quickly.

Hold 'Em...
Accountable

Our lives are a sum total of the choices we have made.

Dr. Wayne Dyer

Three simple choices are available to each of us as leaders. These choices are also a wonderful tool for managing others. Brilliant leaders hold themselves accountable to these choices and use them to hold others accountable.

The three choices we can make in any situation are that we can accept, change, or leave.

When people behave negatively it is often because they believe that they do not have the ability to change their situation. Our job as leaders is to remind ourselves and our teams of the three choices and to employ these choices as an accountability tool.

For example, if you have an employee who is consistently negative you can meet with that employee and explain his or her choices. It might look like this:

Team leader: "Jane, we have talked before about team commitment and at the last team meeting you made negative comments about the upcoming project—I need everyone to be committed to the team's projects."

Jane: "What comments did I make that were perceived as negative?"

Leader: "That you didn't think the project had a hope."

Jane: "Well, I guess I did say that."

Leader: "Are you happy being on this team?"

Jane: "No, not really."

Leader: "Jane, we all have three choices when we are unhappy. We can accept it, change it or make the choice to leave. Accept means you move forward without further negative comments. Change means you are willing to shift your attitude or behaviour to make a difference. Or if you are really that unhappy we can look together at what you would rather be doing and where."

It is important when providing the three choices to avoid communicating them negatively or using them as threats. We want to maintain a caring and concerned attitude while holding the other person accountable to the choices.

Action

- Use the three choices for yourself and hold yourself accountable for the choices you make.
- Use the three choices when dealing with team members to remind them that they are not powerless but powerful.

Why You'll Love It

It feels good to walk your talk! It builds your confidence in your own abilities and it is leadership explicitly demonstrated—others want to follow.

Why They'll Love It

When leaders are seen to hold themselves accountable it inspires others to want to emulate that behaviour.

10 Ignite, Excite, Invite

The important thing to remember is that if you don't have that inspired enthusiasm that is contagious, whatever you do have is also contagious.

Danny Cox

Your team and its performance are a direct reflection of you as a leader. Well-rounded leaders understand the need to be engaged and excited to motivate the members of the team.

Leaders need to share enthusiasm with chutzpah, joie de vivre and sexiness. Gone are the days of the leader who morosely and seriously guided the team to success. Energy in equals energy out, which means if you want the people around you to show excitement and interest then you better darn well be demonstrating the very qualities that you want others to adopt.

Old-style leadership used the motto, "Do as I say, not as I do." New leadership's motto is, "I will do as I say so that you will naturally want to follow me."

Your natural leadership style may not lend itself to vibrant displays of excitement. You may find "motivational" methods uncomfortable or even a bit schmaltzy, but remember that there will be people on your team who are looking for energy, fun and excitement to stay focused and motivated. We want to adapt our leadership style so we can increase the likelihood of buy-in from all personality types. This does not mean we need to be insincere or non-authentic: we simply need to be willing to improve our ability to relate to different perspectives.

In the areas where we just don't feel we have the gift or skill set we have a perfect opportunity to engage others to help us bring that quality to the team. Ask members of your team who are naturally geared towards fun and excitement to conduct team training or to supply humorous ice-breakers before your regular team meetings. The key is that fun has to be an element in the workplace today.

Action

- Do a fun exercise at an upcoming meeting that allows everyone to share a laugh together as a team.

- Put together a funny electronic presentation on the daily challenges within your team. Make jokes about the trials and tribulations that all of you face.
- Create a "fun committee". Ask two or three of your employees to come up with ways to make the workplace fun—rotate the task so everyone participates.
- For a staff special event bring in a caricature artist to do cartoons of the team players and post them in the work area.
- Use self-effacing humour when sending or replying to e-mails—lighten it up!

Why You'll Love It

Having fun alleviates stress, lightens the mood, and increases morale and productivity.

Why They'll Love It

A 1998 survey by the American Management Association stated that employee satisfaction and retention is increased in workplaces that incorporate fun into the daily work environment.

Motivate the
Motivator

. . . .
Motivation is a fire from within. If someone else tries to light
that fire under you, chances are it will burn very briefly.

Stephen Covey

. . . .

Okay, you may have just read #10 and thought to
yourself, "How the heck can I be enthusiastic for my people
when I am having a hard time getting enthused myself?"

If so, you are likely suffering from one of three things.

1. You are bored with your job and can't get excited to get
   out of bed, let alone get up and dressed for work.
2. You are sick and tired of coming up with great ideas
   that are squashed by your boss, so you've lost energy
   for sharing corporate ideas with your team.
3. You have a negative, cynical boss who constantly

complains to you about what's wrong rather than enthusing about what's right.

If any of these three apply, you will definitely have a difficult time motivating others. These are realities that all leaders have either faced or are currently facing. We can choose to let them victimize us or we can rise above them and seek support from other sources so that we can remain motivated and focused.

Many leaders are now hiring personal coaches to support them in their leadership. Coaches support leaders with motivation and leadership ideas, and provide career guidance and counselling. There are even ways to manage your boss (see item #12) so that you can be motivated to lead in the most effective way possible.

Have you ever noticed that when you really believe in something that it is very easy to sell it to others? That's motivation.

As leaders we can become burdened with constantly putting out fires and in the meantime we lose our own!

Action

- Build your own support system. Create a mastermind group with two or three other leaders who you can phone, e-mail and meet to discuss leadership challenges, ideas and solutions.

- Take regular breaks. You are no good to anyone if you end up seriously ill. Pay attention to your fatigue factor and give in to rest if you need it.
- If you don't have a mentor—find one! The value of a mentor is immeasurable for support, guidance and perspective.
- Hire a personal coach for a ninety-day period to re-ignite your excitement for your job and generate new ideas.

Why You'll Love It

Leadership support helps you "fill your cup" with motivation. When you are motivated you are able to support others at a higher level. Seeking support shows your team that you are willing to invest time and money in being a better leader for them.

Why They'll Love It

When you demonstrate your newfound excitement it is naturally contagious. The team's performance increases, morale goes up, and bottom-line results improve for the company.

Managing Your Boss

Winners make their goals; losers make excuses.

Nido Qubein

To be the best leaders we can be we need to not only manage our teams, we need to manage all of our relationships—including the one we have with our boss. If we use our boss as an excuse for our own non-performance we are replacing a victor mentality with a victim mentality. Leaders with a victor mentality choose to take action with communication and clearly-stated expectations. Complaining about the boss's lack of ability, or putting the boss down to our peers or employees, indicates a victim mentality. Negative gossip in any form is not leadership in action.

So what do you do if you do not respect or like your boss? Go back to item #9. You may need to make the "leave it" choice.

Action

- Request that your boss completely support you in your leadership role. Be specific about what that support would look like, such as "I want your commitment that if one of my employees comes to you first that you will redirect them to me."

- Ask your boss to meet with you on a weekly basis to review your goals. Ask that he or she provide you with resources and tools to do your job at the highest level possible.

- Establish a training budget for you and your team, and request full autonomy to manage your team's training requirements.

- Create rapport with your boss by going for coffee or lunch. Ask for time to have frank discussions about challenges or ideas.

- Always think of solutions before approaching your boss with challenges. Make sure your boss knows that you're doing this. You hate it when your team consistently brings you problems, and your boss hates it too!

Why You'll Love It

Communicating openly with your boss about his or her expectations, your expectations, and meeting each other's needs provides a solid foundation from which you can lead at a highly effective level.

Why They'll Love It

Your team will see the rapport and mutual respect between you and your boss and will note that you stand as a unified leadership team. This sends a message of congruent leadership, focused direction and unified goals, which is highly motivating.

Can't Please Everyone All the Time

Crisis can often have value because it generates transformation...
I have found that I always learn more from my mistakes than
from my successes. If you aren't making some mistakes, you aren't
taking enough chances.

John Sculley

The strongest leaders get over the need to be liked. Strong
leaders learn to not take things personally.

When I began leading people I wanted everyone to like
me, so I diluted my opinions and did not stand up for what I
believed in or wanted. The result was that people saw me as
lacking conviction and began to play on my insecurity. It wasn't
until a colleague whose opinion I value asked me, "Why are
you trying so hard to get everybody to like you?" that I realized

42   I had been wasting my energy doing just that. When I changed my approach to fairness and focusing on what was best for the company and the team I earned greater respect and I suffered less stress. In the end one or two people still did not have me on their favourite-person list. I was okay with that.

Our need to be liked is ego-based. It's not the ego itself that is bad because ego drives ambition and accomplishment. Ego only gives us trouble when we succumb to feeding its needs instead of doing what's right for the overall goal.

Ego can also get in the way when we have made a mistake and are unwilling to admit it, for fear that we may be viewed negatively. We all learn from our mistakes and leaders who admit theirs are viewed as human and accountable.

It is difficult to not take things personally, especially when we have a vested interest in seeing our leadership and ideas succeed. I have learned that when my ideas are not embraced, it is not personal. It is about focusing on common goals.

Action

- Check in with yourself by asking the following questions:
   Do I worry about what my team members think of my decisions?

> Am I overly concerned with getting the approval of one particular team member? Why?
>
> Do I waffle or lack conviction when communicating decisions or direction?

- If you answered yes to any of these questions you may be caught in the trap of trying to please all of your people all of the time.

The best way to handle someone who is not pleased with a decision you have made is to re-affirm your confidence in your decision and its benefits to the overall team and company.

Why You'll Love It

When you worry less about being liked, you will find you will have more confidence in your decisions and leadership.

Why They'll Love It

As the team notices that you are taking firmer stands on decisions while acknowledging that not everyone may be happy with them, you are demonstrating your willingness to risk being unpopular. This increases respect for your leadership.

14 Build Employee Loyalty

I leave you with the one piece of advice which I believe will contribute more to making you a better leader, will provide you with greater happiness and self-esteem, and at the same time advance your career more than any other advice that I can provide you. And it doesn't call for special personality or for any certain chemistry. Any one of you can do it. And that advice is: You must care.

Lieutenant General Zais

Statistics state that there will be a shortage of skilled workers by the year 2010. Also, a recent article in the *Harvard Business Review* noted that employees today are not loyal to a company brand but to individuals they work with. This is a shift away from the workplace experience in much of the twentieth century, where workers were completely loyal to a company name.

Downsizing and lay-offs have contributed to this change. Generation X (workers thirty-five and under) specifically adheres to personal loyalty over company loyalty. Gen Xers are more concerned with liking the people they work with than whether the company itself is a brand they are proud to be working for.

The implication for leadership is that building relationships with employees is an important aspect of building loyalty.

Employees don't leave organizations, they leave managers or supervisors. Employees may join an organization for its leadership, good benefits or interesting work, but how long they stay is a function of the relationship with their immediate supervisor or manager.

Research by the Rockhurst University Continuing Education Center in Kansas City, Missouri found five key elements to employee loyalty.

1. Relationships

Employees value leaders who take time to get to know employees as individuals, use work time for special activities such as a holiday lunch, team events or celebrations, and help employees network with other individuals within the organization.

2. Purpose, or meaningful work

    Employees like to see their work tied to the organization's mission and objectives.

3. Competence

    Employees appreciate it when their supervisors provide training and skill development.

4. Achievement

    Leaders who set goals, and make them realistic and measurable, are valued.

5. Recognition

    Employees favour superiors who praise often and implement a rewards program.

Action

- The items listed above are linked to employee retention. Recognize that the employees you risk losing are your top performers. Identify them; build a plan to retain them.

Why You'll Love It

By focusing on employee loyalty you are saving the company thousands of dollars in hiring and re-training.

Why They'll Love It

Employees working for leaders who actively maintain a personal relationship with them tend to feel valued.

Be a Leader
with a Cause

Few will have the greatness to bend history itself, but each of us can work to change a small portion of events... it is from numberless acts of courage and belief that human history is shaped.

Robert F Kennedy

Leaders can sometimes feel trapped by structure. If you are a leader in a corporate environment you may feel handcuffed by business policies and hierarchies that limit your ability to do what you think would really make a difference. Or, if self-employed, you might be frustrated by market conditions or the competition. If you are a leader of an association on a voluntary basis you may feel limited by time.

Let's face it, the reality of any work environment is that

there are restrictions and limitations. But if we focus on limitations we may unconsciously transfer our frustration to our teams.

As a leader with a cause you maintain a strong commitment to work within the limitations, but also to fight for what you need to improve team output or for the greater good of the company as a whole. Team members are inspired by leaders who are willing to be creative, and who view limitations as guidelines for innovative ideas and collaborative solutions.

So instead of focusing on limitations we can focus on what we can control. Things we can't control include:

- Global events
- Corporate policies
- Death
- Taxes.

Many things we do have control over, like:

- Working together
- Communicating in a way that builds results and commitment
- Focusing on what works
- Emphasizing the future and creating solutions

- Being happy with the choices we've made
- Committing to customer care
- Building a happy and functional team.

We need to be leaders with a cause. Courage and conviction come from focusing on what we control and communicating positive alternatives to handling limitations. People will follow leaders to the edge of the earth when it's obvious that external limitations don't stop them from moving forward.

Action

- Ask yourself:

  What is my overall cause?

  What are the limitations I believe are holding me or my team back?

  How can I creatively work around those limitations and communicate to my team that I choose to focus on the cause?

Why You'll Love It

You will have greater confidence and more energy if you focus on what you can control. When you are committed to a cause it allows you to lead from solid business principles.

Why They'll Love It

Energy is contagious! When others witness your willingness to work towards solutions while acknowledging challenges they will join the cause, increasing their commitment to the team as well as their personal loyalty to you.

16 Build Your Dream Team

Let's try winning and see what it feels like. If we don't like it, we can go back to our traditions.

Paul Tsongas

One of the joys of being a leader is that job satisfaction can come from building teams and inspiring others. Many of us were promoted from jobs that were mostly task-based, where our sense of satisfaction came from checking things off our to-do lists.

When we move into leadership, the first few months can be tough as we struggle to find a new source of job satisfaction. A leader's results are actually attained by other people, and are a little less tangible than those in non-management.

Leadership is often so project-based that it may take

months or even years before we can complete a large task. We can feel like we are getting absolutely nothing done. But we *are* getting something done: a leader is as good as the team he or she builds. Key concepts to building your dream team are:

- Hire them right in the first place. Outline the roles of each of your team players, and plan your hiring around projects and the dynamics of your group.
- Hire for attitude. A good attitude cannot be taught, but skills can.
- Build a diverse team. Mix up the personality styles so that your team fosters creativity with differing perspectives.
- For existing team members, determine who are your:

  "A" employees—the ones you don't want to lose. These need mentoring and motivation.

  "B" employees, who need guidance and training.

  "C" employees. These need disciplinary action or to be relocated.

Action

- Imagine your team-leader role as the coach of a sports team. Ask yourself questions like:

What do I want the team to accomplish?

What would indicate our success?

Which people would be most suited for specific projects?

Who would grow from taking on a specific project?

What team rewards could I put into place to recognize team effort?

Building your dream team requires a consistent time investment in coaching as well as constant communication of expectations and feedback.

Why You'll Love It

Leaders have a direct role in building and developing a team that is a joy to work with. When you plan and build your team around the results you want to create, you are more likely to pair the right people with the right tasks and create greater team satisfaction.

Why They'll Love It

A team that knows it is part of a grand plan to reach a common goal tends to function more cooperatively. When each person on the team understands his or her role and is recognized for it, individual contribution increases.

Thanks and Praise

A person may not be as good as you tell her she is, but she'll try harder thereafter.

Anonymous

What costs a leader nothing but gives immeasurable return? Praise and recognition.

A simple thank-you for a job well done, a few words of encouragement, or a public announcement to peers can go a very long way.

The key to effective praise is the way it is delivered. To ensure that praise is well received it must be:

- Specific—what did they do exactly?
- Sincere—eye contact, handshake or hug if appropriate
- Customized—a handwritten card, an e-mail announcement or a team announcement, depending on the employee's personality style.

Do not underestimate the power of delegating recognition. Delegate assignments that allow an employee to shine and you will find that the employee will become even more loyal.

A leader I knew in a financial institution had a very outgoing employee who wanted to get involved in public relations. The leader was asked to be the subject of a magazine interview about best practices within the HR department, but instead asked her employee if she wanted to be interviewed. The employee was honoured, thrilled and flattered, and not only did the interview go very successfully but she worked even harder than before.

Action

- Identify an employee, peer or colleague who you can recognize for his or her contributions.
- Recognize that person in a unique way that honours his or her preferences, hobbies or personality.
- Have a meeting with your team and recognize each of them publicly for their contributions to the team's successes. You can also turn this into a team activity by having the group identify one another's contributions publicly.

Why You'll Love It

It's easier to give thanks and praise than you might think. You may feel that it is unnecessary to thank others for every little thing, but when you get into the habit of recognizing good things people are doing it sets a tone of encouragement and willingness to risk. You feel better because you are focusing on what they are doing right instead of complaining about things that are not being done well.

Why They'll Love It

What's not to like? Many employees feel taken for granted. When you praise or recognize them it validates their contributions. Praise creates greater employee satisfaction and decreases employee turnover.

It's About Time

Time is everything. Anything you want, anything you accomplish—pleasure, success, fortune—is measured in time.

Joyce C Hall

Recent management surveys indicate that people would prefer a more flexible work environment and more time off than more money. Think about it. Would you rather receive a 5 percent pay increase that gets swallowed by taxes or some time off that allows you to catch up on personal things?

Many of us find that there isn't enough time in the day. Stress levels increase, our personal lives suffer, and eventually our work suffers as we struggle to juggle our time.

As companies downsize, the number of people working has decreased while expectations for productivity have increased. If we as leaders do not recognize the need for our teams to have personal time off we risk burning them out—and this applies to ourselves too!

Flexibility creates loyalty: more companies are offering a four-day work week, flex time or every second Friday off.

Action

While you need to consider conditions or restrictions specific to your situation, think about these opportunities to add flexibility to the workplace.

- Could you reward a top performer by letting him or her have half a Friday off?
- Could you introduce rotating time-off periods based on team performance?
- As an incentive for a major project could you put up an extra week of vacation time as a reward?
- What other options are available in your company to provide flexibility to your employees?

Why You'll Love It

Include yourself in the time-off incentive plan. When you have extra time you feel better equipped to deal with the stresses and demands of the job.

Why They'll Love It

Employees who feel valued and respected enough to be given extra personal time tend to work harder, remain loyal and keep an upbeat and optimistic attitude.

Do a 360!

In old-style leadership, the leader evaluated employees'
performance based on the leader's limited exposure to the
employees' work habits. This one-sided perspective on
performance could de-motivate instead of inspiring employees
to higher levels of performance.

A new leadership performance evaluation tool is the 360-
degree review. The employee evaluates his or her performance,
the leader completes the standard review and assessment,
and then two or three peers evaluate the employee as well.
Some companies are taking the concept one step further and
including client assessments as part of the overall employee
review process. The result is a panoramic view of individual

performance that outlines strengths and areas for improvement.

It is difficult to dispute an assessment when more than one person notes an area for improvement. The keys to success with 360 reviews are training everyone in the skill of giving effective feedback, and positioning the review process as a positive growth tool.

Action

- Do a leadership assessment on yourself! Create a one-page form of specific questions on your skills for your team and peers to complete.
- You can decide if you want the process to be anonymous. It depends on your comfort level and that of your team and peers. Just make sure you do not punish anyone as a result of the feedback you get!
- After receiving the feedback have a meeting to thank them for it and make a commitment to work on the areas mentioned for improvement.
- Introduce 360 in your next performance reviews by asking employees to self-evaluate and then having two or three other employees evaluate them as well.
- For more information on 360s search with the keywords

"360 performance reviews", or check out the Web site www.assessments.biz.

Why You'll Love It

Going through the 360 yourself is an eye-opener. When you become aware of new areas for improvement, your performance level increases.

Why They'll Love It

By going through the process you are demonstrating your willingness to hear feedback. This makes it more comfortable for your employees too. When peers evaluate each other in constructive and supportive ways team members become more accountable to each other.

Coach for Success

Outstanding leaders go out of their way to boost the self-esteem of their personnel. If people believe in themselves, it's amazing what they can accomplish.

Sam Walton

Many leaders have mismatched expectations about their teams' abilities and the output desired. We can't assume that they know everything to do their jobs at the highest level, so we want to provide constant and consistent support for learning in our teams. Studies have shown that loyalty increases when employees feel that they are constantly learning and growing on the job, and coaching is the easiest way to encourage learning.

Coaching is different than managing. Coaching is creating an environment where others figure things out for themselves, feel safe making decisions, and learn and grow in the process.

Managing is when the leader autocratically gives the answers all of the time, which does not allow creative brainstorming or team involvement. We want to coach if we want to create autonomous and self-directed work teams.

Action

- Build a coaching plan that consists of the following:

    A gap analysis of each employee, listing the current skill levels of the employee and what is required to do his or her job at the highest level. Now, where are the gaps in knowledge and ability?

    An ongoing coaching program. Set it up in ninety-day segments per employee.

    Let them choose courses to attend.

    Build a learning library that has books, tapes and workbooks on various skill sets.

    Provide employees with non-library tools and resources, such as where to look or who to call for specific kinds of information. You can follow up as part of the coaching plan.

Why You'll Love It

Ongoing coaching gives you a greater sense of control

over the direction of the team and a hand in the performance improvement of each employee. You will enjoy greater satisfaction in building up your people, and less stress.

Why They'll Love It

Coaching is personalized development and training that every employee wants. Studies have proven that employees who are coached perform at higher levels, have greater job satisfaction, and show increased loyalty to their leader.

Talking 'bout My Generation

21

There are four stages of humankind: infancy... childhood... adolescence... and obsolescence.

Art Linkletter

Generational awareness is a must for effective and less-stressed leaders. The differing values and attitudes of each generation can create a work environment filled with miscommunication and conflict.

Each generation has unique perspectives shaped by its environment, and the more leaders can learn to identify the range of generational viewpoints the more creatively we can lead. We need to be aware of four distinct generations in the workplace.

The Veteran age group is generally fifty-five and older. This generation is post-World War II and its nature is to be loyal to a single employer. Veterans expect the same loyalty to be displayed towards them. Veterans tend to be frugal and do not understand using debt to build business or the need for anyone to have debt at all. In the workplace they show up on time and they take orders—they do as they are told and they respect their bosses as well as their elders, even if they disagree with them.

The Baby Boomer age group is generally thirty-five to fifty-four: these are the children of the Veterans. They grew up with little in the way of toys or nice clothes and vowed to give their children everything they couldn't have. In most cases Baby Boomers understand the principle of working to earn a living. They probably left home at the age of eighteen and survival was a real issue. At work, if you tell Baby Boomers to do something or they will be fired, they will usually do it because they are afraid of not being able to pay the bills. In the workplace they have a mentality of work, work, and work… and then you die.

Generation Xers are typically the twenty-three to thirty-four-year-old children of the Baby Boomers. In many cases both parents worked while Generation X grew up, and Gen X saw their Baby Boomer parents get laid off or witnessed them being miserable in their jobs. This helped shape their current value system, which is, "I am going to have a life first and work will come second." It is Generation X who is pushing for flex hours, four-day work weeks, paid sabbaticals for education and paid parental leave for both fathers and mothers. In the workplace you cannot threaten Gen Xs with firing to get them to do something because they don't care. Statistics show that most Generation Xs live at home until the age of twenty-six and do not have the same survival issues that the Baby Boomers had. Their main goal is to have fun at work, make a buck and have a life.

Generation Y is twenty-two and younger. I think they are called Generation Y because that is the question they often ask: "Why?" They may be the younger brothers and sisters of Gen X or children of Gen X, and so far are one of the most creative generations we have seen in a long time. Generation Ys want to work where they are allowed creative expression, a flexible approach and control over their own hours. In the workplace they show little loyalty because they know they will have ten or more careers in their lifetimes. They get bored very quickly and need other incentives besides a paycheque.

What generational differences imply is that we cannot apply one style of leadership to motivate our teams to create results. We need to include generational differences and their impact on work teams in our awareness of our employees.

Action

- Identify the composition of your team from a generational standpoint.
- What generation makes up the majority of your team?
- Research how to motivate the different generations—there are many resources on the Web if you type "motivating the generations" or "generations at work" into a search engine.
- Hold a team training event to raise awareness of generational value differences. Discuss how each age group approaches its work and how the team can build greater respect among the generations.

Why You'll Love It

Broadening your awareness of the mindsets of the generations and how they approach their work helps you delegate, motivate, and encourage the team to greater performance.

Why They'll Love It

Each age group will appreciate that its work approach is valued for what it brings to the team dynamic.

Give 'Em the Goods

Accomplishment will prove to be a journey, not a destination.

Dwight D Eisenhower

The general public mistrusts executives of large companies—just say "Enron" and people shake their heads. It seems more and more difficult to find leaders who are willing to tell the truth to their shareholders, management teams and employees.

We *want* the truth. Don't BS us, don't try to sugar-coat what's going on—give us the goods.

Many leaders that I have worked with say, "We don't need to tell them this until... " My advice is always to address issues right away because it is likely that the employees already know something about what the executives don't want to announce. More damage can be done by not admitting the truth—employees begin to speculate, gossip and assume, which can deflate morale in a heartbeat.

When employees are given information, negative or positive, they feel part of what's going on. They feel empowered to make decisions for themselves.

I once worked with a construction client while it reorganized. The sales process was going to be affected, but the owner did not want to communicate that to the sales team immediately because he didn't want to alarm them. I suggested that we hold a team sales meeting to address the current situation and to gather ideas on improving sales. During the meeting, management could bring up proposed sales process changes and outline their benefits—the need for change would already have been established in the meeting by the sales team itself so the likelihood of acceptance was quite high. The executive agreed, and asked me to facilitate the meeting.

At the meeting the natural evolution of the discussion led the group to the conclusion that changes were needed. We then discussed the proposed changes, which were indeed readily accepted.

As leaders our desire to hold back the truth is based on

74 fear of conflict or the belief that "too much knowledge is a bad thing". A master leader doesn't fear the truth; rather he or she considers how best to deliver it compassionately, with focus and in a way that it will truly be heard.

Action

- Identify items currently the subject of gossip or speculation within the team and meet to address these.
- In your one-on-one coaching with your team members, address rumours and encourage your employees to ask for clarification on things they have heard.

Why You'll Love It

The truth is much easier to remember! It is less stressful and allows you to lead with integrity. You worry less about being liked and concentrate more on being fair and truthful.

Why They'll Love It

A management survey conducted by Rockhurst University asked managers for the number-one quality they appreciate in their leaders. Leaders who tell the truth were at the top of the list. Your team will appreciate your honesty and work harder knowing they are being kept in the loop.

What's Your Succession Plan?

Business more than any other occupation is a continual dealing with the future: it is a continual calculation, an instinctive exercise in foresight.

Henry R Luce

Who will take over when you move on? No leader is completely indispensable. Master leaders plan for the future and have identified one or two people who could easily move into their leadership role.

We need to feel secure enough in our abilities that we will happily groom someone to take over from us. We can do it because we know that when the day comes we will be moving on to something else, and we know that we do not need to feel threatened by our team.

Succession planning is a proactive investment in the well-being of the company, and a master leader's commitment is to the legacy of the business—with or without him or her.

A home-builder client of mine brought this point home to me in a dramatic fashion. The COO was a well-respected and well-liked gentleman. The company shares were at an all-time high, customers were happy with delivery... And then he had a heart attack.

The entire company stopped in its tracks. There had been no knowledge transfer to future VPs, and although there had been informal acknowledgement of future VPs nothing had been put in writing. Thankfully the COO recovered, and as soon as he was back at work the executive team met and drew up a five, ten and fifteen-year succession plan. Think of a succession plan as a will for your business.

Action

- Identify at least two people who show promise in replacing you if you were to leave.
- In their coaching sessions let them know you see their potential and want to mentor and guide them for the role someday.

- Build their coaching plans around the skills they will
  need to fulfill the role.

The strongest leaders build a legacy for peace of mind; it's like a retirement fund. You have planned for the future and yet are secure in your current role.

Why You'll Love It

Building a succession plan is a career plan for you as well. If forces you to look at where you see yourself in the next few years and also allows you to coach potential leaders at a higher level. It is rewarding to groom someone to replace you.

Why They'll Love It

When a team sees that the leader has the foresight to plan for the future, pride is developed within the company. It also creates healthy competition among team members to perform at the highest levels possible.

Lead with Quiet Confidence

Who transforms businesses when a company must patiently, day by day, strive towards its passionately desired future? It's the unsung—and decidedly unglamorous—heroes who deserve credit for these feats.

Jim Collins for the Harvard Business Review

Jim Collins, the author of *Good to Great* (HarperCollins, 2001) identified a key characteristic of leaders of companies that were considered consistently great. They were not charismatic and loud. Rather, they were humble and unassuming.

I worked for a mortgage insurance company in the late '80s as an area sales manager. My boss there, who I will call Dana, was dynamic and a well-respected leader. I wanted to be just like her one day.

I worked hard for her and wanted to demonstrate my abilities. After about six months she invited me in to her office for an informal chat. She asked me how I was enjoying my team and our results and then quietly asked me what we had been working on. I began to boast about our increased sales figures and the accounts I had personally obtained. She smiled and made a memorable statement. "Cheryl, there is something to be said for quiet confidence. As a leader you don't need to continually tell your team or me what you have personally done. The results speak for themselves. I would like to see you practice being less 'out there' with your accomplishments—let your accomplishments shout for you."

Wow, well said. It caused me to re-evaluate my leadership style. Although it was difficult to hear the feedback, I now view it as invaluable in shaping my abilities as a leader.

Quiet confidence is developed when we work towards major goals, give credit to our team instead of taking credit ourselves, and let go of the need to ensure everyone knows about the level of our contribution as a leader.

Action

- The next time you feel the urge to brag about what you accomplished, point out an accomplishment the team or a specific individual has made.

- Keep a log at work of all your accomplishments. Record them for your performance review, where it is perfectly appropriate to toot your own horn.

Why You'll Love It

Quiet confidence is liberating because you are completely secure in your abilities, calm and humble.

Why They'll Love It

Your team will respect and admire you for not taking credit for the team's accomplishments. You will find you will receive more support and compliments from the team as they feel more secure and safe under your leadership.

Count the Cost of Non~Performance

Our strengths are our tools, our personal reality. Our weaknesses are only what we are not.

Joe Batten

There isn't a company out there who can afford to have a team member who is not contributing at a high level. As leaders we can do all the right things with our team—we can motivate, reward and inspire. But by not dealing with a challenging employee we can defeat everything we have built.

When a team sees that an underperforming employee is getting away with low performance it completely brings down morale for the entire team. The attitude that quickly permeates the team is one of "Why bother? If Jack can get away with not doing his share why should I bust my buns?"

Many leaders postpone discussing performance with these employees because confrontational discussions can be uncomfortable. It takes a lot of energy to deal with a challenging person so we often procrastinate. But deal with it we must, or the benefits of all of our other positive efforts to build team and morale will go out the window.

Action

- Identify your "hostage takers": these are the employees who are negative, often absent, and poor performers. They hold workplaces hostage by getting away with negative behaviours.
- Address the behaviours directly with these employees and hold them accountable for change.
- Approach the conversation with a positive attitude. Ensure you are clear in advance of the meeting on what the employee is doing now that is not correct, what you need him or her to do, and by when—be specific.
- Let the employee know the full disciplinary process that your organization uses, such as:

    Step One—verbal warning

    Step Two—written warning

    Step Three—second written warning

Step Four—agreement to help them find work that is more suitable.

- Explain your commitment to helping the employee succeed and remind him or her of the three choices we discussed in #9 earlier.

Why You'll Love It

Imagine the sigh of relief when you deal with a challenging employee. You will feel better, and although it can be stressful to confront a problem it is more stressful to procrastinate.

Why They'll Love It

Employees often feel that nothing is done about non-performance. When they see that you are consistent and fair in addressing performance they respond by working harder.

Give Effective Feedback

I have my faults. But being wrong ain't one of them.

Jimmy Hoffa

The most powerful motivational tool out there is already available. Because it is too simple we may simply overlook it and not use it as often as we could. That tool is feedback.

There is a direct correlation between feedback and performance. Often we are so busy that ongoing effective coaching using feedback gets put on the back burner.

Generations X and Y have a strong need for positive feedback. Some of you reading this may be saying, "Give me a break! Whatever happened to just doing your job?" Notice that those of us saying that are typically Baby Boomers or

Veterans. The younger generations expect to receive ongoing recognition and feedback.

Giving effective feedback is also an excellent accountability tool because it outlines expectations for improving performance and asks for an action plan on how workers are going to accomplish goals.

For feedback to be effective it needs to be:

- Timely
- Specific
- Focused on the future
- Action-oriented
- Followed up.

Here's an example.

"Jane, I have noticed that when you take on a project you are excellent at initiating excitement at the beginning and then you seem to lose interest and focus once it is started. Next time you begin a project it would help if you were to use a planning process such as a spreadsheet with update checkpoints that allow you and your team to keep the momentum going. What do you need to ensure this happens with the next project?"

With this scenario let's assume Jane needs spreadsheet training or support from you. Both of those items would be part of the follow-up.

Effective feedback is always about improving performance while at the same time motivating the other person to do better, learn more and grow in the process.

Action

- Use the "sandwich" technique the next time you give feedback to anyone. It is:
    1. Open with a positive statement.
    2. Specifically state what they are doing now and what you want them to do in the future.
    3. Ask what they need to make the change, and a commitment to change or improve.
    4. Close with a positive statement about their ability to follow through on the feedback.

Why You'll Love It

Feedback improves performance, which frees up your time and relieves stress.

Why They'll Love It

Performance cannot be improved without knowing what needs to be done. Nothing is worse for an employee than not knowing what needs to be improved and then getting penalized come performance review time.

27 Stop the Blame Game

Happiness depends upon ourselves.

Aristotle

It's a challenge for many team leaders to eliminate the blame game in the workplace. Positive energy is created when each individual is accountable and responsible.

Leaders can become frustrated when employees, co-workers and even bosses do not take personal responsibility, choosing to blame a person or circumstance instead. Try evaluating yourself with these questions.

- Do I look at my part in the problem and take responsibility for what I have full control over?
- Do I lead by choices or do I find myself blaming the company, the boss or the team?

- Do I reward my team for taking responsibility and for not playing the blame game?

Remember that we cannot be sure that everyone knows what the rules are unless we communicate expectations. Leaders who have communicated the rules of the game to their departments and teams feel less like glorified babysitters.

Action

- When coaching each employee include accountability and what it looks like:

    Before blaming, investigate the situation thoroughly.

    Do all you can to communicate, explain and understand a situation before laying blame.

    Approach the person who may have caused the problem (in a non-confrontational way) to build solutions, not conflicts.

    Communicate your needs and expectations for future situations to the other person.

- Set ground rules for conduct and behaviour. Establish a safe zone for making mistakes and taking blame. Post it in the office as a reminder of accountability for the team.

- Encourage the team to peer-coach each other: if they catch a co-worker blaming something or someone else, they give a signal to remind them to focus on a solution rather than on who or what caused the problem in the first place.

Why You'll Love It

Creating an accountable team removes a tremendous amount of stress and minimizes gossip, finger-pointing and loss of productivity.

Why They'll Love It

When individuals are held accountable they strive to partner with others in building creative solutions, instead of focusing on the problem and blaming contributing factors.

Keep on the Right Track

In all things, success depends upon previous preparation, and without such preparation, there is sure to be failure.

Confucius

When employees surveyed by the American Management Association were asked how they felt about meetings, their comments were telling: "What a waste of time." "Here we go again." "No one does what they say they will in a meeting anyway." "It's just a chance for everyone to gather and complain."

These are pretty cynical yet honest comments and in some cases they are true. As leaders we cannot afford to waste time on ineffective meetings. Each meeting we plan needs to have a specific purpose, agenda and call to action.

Holding effective meetings is fairly easy to do but requires strong facilitation skills. The facilitator needs to ensure that ground rules and codes of conduct are followed to keep the meeting moving. An example of ground rules that could be pre-written on a whiteboard or flip chart are:

1. We will stick to the agenda.
2. If you have thoughts or questions that are not pertinent to the immediate discussion please write them down and we will tackle them later if we have time, or we can discuss them one-on-one after the meeting.

Keep in mind that different personality styles have different needs, so it is important to incorporate a fun icebreaker, a brief opportunity to network as peers and then move to the meat of the meeting, ending with commitment and action.

It is our job to follow up on outstanding action items and to create a forum for reporting back to the group. One way to do that is to create an intranet forum specifically for task forces and teams to report information and action on specific projects.

Action

- Go over the ground rules before getting down to business—make it an agenda item.
- Establish a way to ensure that everyone is heard without censure. One way to do this is to use a "talking stick" like many aboriginal peoples do. The person holding the stick may speak without interruption.
- Remind your team that the meeting's goal is to come up with concrete ideas and action. This will require commitment and follow-through, and direct reporting back to the group by specific dates.

Why You'll Love It

Holding meetings will feel less like a chore if you set up each meeting with a specific focus, agenda and expected action.

Why They'll Love It

No more whining about how ineffective meetings are! Well, that's not entirely true—you will never please all people all of the time. But the majority of your team will appreciate the efficiency and creativity you bring to meetings.

Lighten Up!

Why humour? Why not humour? I'd rather it be my ally than my enemy.

Robert Orben

What if work was more *fun*? Southwest Airlines' CEO Herb Kelleher says, "If work was more fun, it would feel less like work." Companies like Southwest and Sun Microsystems are realizing the value of creating an enjoyable workplace. The beauty of their vision is that they can create a fun environment *and* remain profitable companies.

In a survey by Robert Half International, 84 percent of the CEOs and Human Resource Directors surveyed indicated that people with a sense of humour do a better job. A study by Hodge Cronin and Associates reported that 98 percent of the 737 CEOs interviewed would prefer to hire someone with a sense of humour over someone without one. Humour can help us develop a psychological distance from potentially stressful situations so that we can deal with them more rationally.

Many Dictator-Driver personality types feel there is no time for fun and games at the office, and Detailers feel that if people are laughing on the job they mustn't be getting anything done. But all work and no play makes for a very dull and uninspired day.

If you have an office full of Dictator types you have lots getting done but ego clashes or power struggles are the norm. If you have an office full of Detailer types it is very quiet and very serious, but people tend to lack energy. An office full of Dancers is a party! A balance of styles is optimal for the workplace. Ideally we want to take the positive qualities of each style and incorporate those into office culture. Dancers do bring levity, fun and silliness to the work environment and add to the "fun" factor.

As leaders we can begin by not taking ourselves so seriously, perhaps by posting a few non-offensive comics or jokes to remind us to have a laugh. Keep things in perspective and help others to lighten up as well.

Action

- Just for fun, do something silly on a Monday morning

like wear funny glasses or a goofy hat. (I can just see the Detailers cringing at this suggestion!)

- The next time you make a mistake, make light of it and poke some fun at yourself—and then find a solution.
- Encourage your team to laugh and tell them you want them to have fun while working hard. Delegate fun to your team: for instance, have them take turns in coming up with fun icebreakers for meetings or creating a fun activity at the end of a particularly stressful week.

Why You'll Love It
What's not to love???
Why They'll Love It
Fun equals energy equals greater job satisfaction.

Customize When You Recognize

Advice is like snow; the softer it falls, the longer it dwells upon, and the deeper it sinks into the mind.

Samuel Taylor Coleridge

Adapt your recognition of others to their personality styles. Dictators want you to give them a tangible reward for a job well done. Dancers want loud recognition: they want everyone to know that they did something wonderful. Put it on the loudspeaker, post it in the lunchroom and send a mass e-mail. Detailers are suspicious of recognition and wonder what your ulterior motive really is, so you need to be up front right away and tell them you are not asking for anything else but simply want to acknowledge the detail and care that went into their work. Deflectors are happy with a quiet thank-you or a handwritten note. Flowers or candy will make them your devoted fan forever.

Hard work is its own reward—or so Baby Boomers and Veterans think. In reality we all need some stroking and recognition to keep plugging along. For the best results use a combination of all four, and create customized reward and recognition programs for your team.

The best recognition programs contain the following:

- Tangible rewards, such as money or time off,
- Visibility, in the form of a picture taken and circulated in a company newsletter or e-mail newsletter,
- Personalized handwritten cards that specifically identify what the person did and the impact it had on the department and overall business success, and
- A thank-you for their continued hard work and recognition of sacrifices made, such as time at home or with family.

Action

- Build a list of recognition items you can provide to your team.
- Ask each team member what he or she would personally like when being recognized.

- Make a list of each person on the team and put individualized recognition ideas beside each name, such as a gift certificate for a golf game for the team member who is a golf lover.
- At every team meeting build in time for kudos and recognition among peers.

Many recognition programs fail or lose impact with employees because they assume that everyone will enjoy the perk. For example, having a pizza day may seem like a fun way to recognize your team but may not interest those who are not pizza lovers, those on low-carb diets, or those who bring their own lunches. It doesn't mean we can't have pizza days; it means we mix up our recognition activities to meet the needs of the individuals in our teams. Customize when you recognize.

Why You'll Love It

If feels good to be thoughtful and to take the time to reward individuals in a way that they want.

Why They'll Love It

When employees or team members are individually

100 recognized it means more. It strikes a personal chord that builds employee loyalty and makes them feel cared for by their team leader.

Share the Limelight

Great leaders know that they can motivate their teams by sharing the limelight. It takes a leader with high self-esteem to be willing to let individuals or teams take the credit for accomplishments.

An executive that I have been coaching is extremely good at this. She recently submitted two of her employees' names to her boss, requesting that her superior personally send them a handwritten card to thank them for their contributions to the team's project success. This leader did not ask to be mentioned as the one making the request. She preferred to keep it anonymous.

The employees were like kids on Christmas morning when they enthusiastically shared what they had received. She never let on that she had initiated it and took great pleasure in their satisfaction.

The impact on her team and the two individuals was very positive and kept the energy and enthusiasm for the next project at an all-time high.

Action

- What information about your team could you provide to your boss for recognition?
- The next time you are praised for your team's performance make sure you pass along the kudos in a team meeting or via e-mail.
- The next time you are given credit, accept and include your team and their contributions.

Why You'll Love It

It feels good to "share the love" with your team and the individuals in it.

Why They'll Love It

When teams feel supported, valued and recognized by their boss, their peers and upper management, it builds a sense of willingness to work harder.

Get Out of the Rut

One of the most courageous things you can do is identify yourself, know who you are, what you believe in, and where you want to go.

Sheila Murray Bethel

It can be boring to do the same old, same old at work. We get restless when things are ticking along at a regular rate. Great leaders strive for excellence, not mediocrity. What can you do that will make you stretch and grow and be bolder with an eye towards excellence? What standards or goals will help you reach a higher plateau of success?

The cycle of success means we reach a milestone or a plateau and then we peter out. If you are feeling lethargic, apathetic and bored it could be because you have reached the plateau blahs.

I had set lofty goals that I wanted to reach before I turned forty this past year. Well, when I realized I had achieved all of them I didn't get excited, I got scared. I was scared because I had an ominous feeling of "now what?"

I realized that once you reach a level of success it is necessary to continue to set new goals and look ahead. I took some time to plan my goals for the next ten years and once again found myself re-focused, re-energized and excited about the future.

To break through the plateau blahs we need to:

- Acknowledge the accomplishments and successes we have had to date.
- Set new personal and professional goals that will challenge us.
- Announce those new goals and standards of excellence to our boss and our team.

A plateau is also a good time to go back to school, attend a conference, or take a course or degree program. Stretch yourself to continue to learn. Effective leaders are lifelong learners.

Action

- Re-write your goals to include goals for the next five years and the next milestone birthday. Include personal as well as professional goals.

- Sign up for a night course in a new language or skill.
- Take a course in art—the *Harvard Business Review* says the degree most valued in today's economy is a Master of Fine Arts!
- Create team goals based on your vision of what your team can do in the next six months and year.
- Communicate those goals to your team. Get buy-in, commitment and excitement from your team about those goals.

Why You'll Love It

Leadership can become boring. When you shake things up you keep your energy levels up and you create positive change. Taking a course or setting new goals can re-ignite the passion for leadership.

Why They'll Love It

Your team and peers will respect you for being unwilling to settle for a certain level of success. It is inspiring to see someone who is continually stretching themselves intellectually toward new goals.

Ain't any Shame
in Taking the Blame

"Eating crow" is never pleasant—no matter how much mustard and ketchup you put on it. But usually the sooner you eat it the less unpleasant it is to the taste!

Anonymous

Whether we admit it or not, people can see right through us. When we do not hold ourselves to the same ideals to which we hold others they become disillusioned with us.

Many leaders lose face when they do not admit fault for something that they personally did or did not do. A respected leader is one who admits fault and then makes suggestions on how to solve the problem.

When we are at fault four simple steps can help us handle it with grace and class.

1. Admit it.
2. Thank them for their tolerance or patience.
3. Explain the circumstances briefly and succinctly.
4. Take responsibility and explain what we will do to resolve the problem.

When we immediately take personal blame and then move to provide a solution there is nothing more to say. If only more politicians would figure this out!

Action

- The next time you say or do something that results in an error or miscommunication simply admit it and follow the steps above.
- Follow up once you have taken action to rectify the situation.
- If a team member tries to cover for you or take the blame, thank them for their concern but step in and own up to it.

Why You'll Love It

When you just 'fess up and get it over with, making a mistake results in less drama and thus less stress.

Why They'll Love It

Your team and peers learn more from your actions than your words. When they see that you readily admit mistakes and take personal responsibility for fixing them, the team feels that they have permission to make mistakes, learn from them, admit them and then provide solutions.

Don't Take It Personally

People need to like you in order to follow you. On the other hand not everyone is going to like you—but go for the majority.

Donald Trump

Being likeable increases your chances for success as a leader because human nature is such that people want to help a likeable person succeed. The reality is, though, that not everyone is going to like you. I bet you can even think of someone in your own family who doesn't like you all that much.

Successful leaders have learned that to be effective you may not always be popular, but you can increase your likeability factor by becoming more aware of and adaptable to others.

Driver-Dictator personalities have an easier time getting over the need to be liked than other personality styles. Their drive for results means they often overlook the need for a softer, more human touch—they tend to not take things personally by their very nature. But if they work on caring more about being liked and increasing their likeability they become even more effective.

Other styles have a more difficult time separating likeability from leadership. The Dancer is a social creature so wants to be popular; the Deflector may have trouble making tough decisions in an effort to try to please everyone; and Detailers are so focused on data and proof that they can assume that their detail makes up for camaraderie.

We can all learn from the Dictator-Driver personality not to take things personally when someone does not like us, or our ideas. It's not personal in most cases; it is simply a difference of opinion, values or personality. For example, an older male colleague may call me "dear", and previously this would have annoyed me. Now I accept that males of the Veteran generation often use endearments. It is not meant to be patronizing—it is an affectation. If it did bother me I would simply address it assertively by asking not to be called "dear".

Our likeability factor goes up when we are less defensive and more open to different perspectives.

Action

- The next time you feel that someone has made a personal dig, clarify it by saying something like, "What did you mean by that?", "Are you trying to hurt my feelings?" or "I'm not sure what that comment is referring to. Can you clarify?" All of these are exploratory questions that will help clear the air.
- Evaluate the overall picture and ask yourself if you are being overly sensitive due to gender differences, personality differences, power struggles or generational differences.

Why You'll Love It

You will find leadership so much more rewarding and enjoyable when you make an effort to understand where others are coming from. Looking for hidden agendas or feeling that people are out to get you is no fun.

Why They'll Love It

When others sense that you do not take things to heart

and that you are able to keep your self-esteem intact, you lead by example. You are not operating from a strong need to be liked but rather from confidence and self-assurance. They respect and admire your ability to be authentic to yourself even if it means not pleasing everyone all of the time.

Let Them Drain Your Brain

A great teacher never strives to explain his vision—he simply invites you to stand beside him and see for yourself.

Reverend E Inman

Leaders who are focused on the future are what I call "legacy leaders". They are looking beyond their immediate impact on their teams, departments and companies, and thinking about the long term.

As mentioned earlier, every strong team has a succession plan in place. In addition strong teams have built-in structures that allow knowledge transfer.

Fully confident leaders are not afraid to share everything they know because they have learned that the more they pass on to their teams the more ability the team can show and the more autonomy it has.

Some leaders I have coached resist sharing knowledge because they admit to being afraid of becoming redundant. That resistance is based on a lack of confidence in their own talents and abilities. Leaders who willingly share what they know often go on to lead even bigger and better teams because they have shown they can lead at a high level.

Regular skills-transfer training from you to your teammates is the best form of "legacy leadership". Ask each of your employees which of your regular duties or tasks they would like to learn to do. Spend a few hours teaching them: let them watch you perform the task and ask questions, then try it themselves. Finally, de-brief the session to fine-tune.

Action

- Set up a cross-training timetable that allows everyone to learn each job within your department.
- Create a learning library in your office: a collection of books, tapes and magazines that employees can take home for further learning. Offer resources when coaching each of them individually.
- Share what you know with your two or three planned successors and have regular mentoring meetings with

them to discuss politics, executive decisions and the thinking behind your decisions.

- Track what you did for specific projects so that information can be passed on when you leave.

Why You'll Love It

As you share what you know you can grow by training your employees. You also free up more time because you can delegate tasks as their knowledge increases.

Why They'll Love It

An American Management Association survey showed that one of the most common employee complaints was that they were not able to spend one-on-one time with the boss in order to learn, ask questions and try something new.

Communication is the Key

The way we communicate with others and with ourselves ultimately determines the quality of our lives.

Anthony Robbins, Unlimited Power

A chef came to a management seminar I was conducting in Santa Monica to learn how to improve the performance of his team. When I brought up the importance of communicating clearly when managing others the chef got downright indignant and said, "I don't have time for that. Shouldn't they just get it? If they don't get it, they're outta here." When asked what his turnover rate was the chef turned red in the face and admitted it was extremely high.

Why? Partly because the restaurant industry as a whole experiences high turnover, but also because leaders often blame the people they hire instead of looking at what they are contributing to the problem.

This chef had asked his sous-chef to make a soufflé and assumed that the soufflé would be made exactly the way he himself did it. When it was not, the chef blew up and belittled his employee. In six weeks he had hired and fired five different sous-chefs! Who do you think was the source of the problem? This chef was a classic Driver-Dictator personality type with little patience for communicating in a different way. He was also impatient with others' learning curves.

We cannot expect that everyone will automatically know what we want, nor can we expect that they will do it perfectly or just like we would. During the seminar I provided some examples of communicating in a clear and direct way while honouring the six steps of successful delegation discussed in #5.

When executives and leaders tell me they don't have time to coach, or to communicate, I wonder what kind of an investment they are making in their employees. The time investment in communicating clearly and coaching is exactly that—an investment—and the results on the other side of that investment are increased employee morale, increased performance and an increased likelihood of loyalty.

Action

- Where could you improve your communication skills?
- Is your leadership style more aggressive or passive?
- If you don't have the patience to teach the skills needed, who on your team could be an effective teacher?

Why You'll Love It

Clear communication saves time, money and effort. Clear understanding means jobs get done the way you want.

Why They'll Love It

Employee morale goes up because the job gets done to your standards as well as to theirs.

Let Them be CEOs

Winning is a reflex action. If you've been there in your mind, you'll go there in your body.

Dennis Waitley

A few weeks ago I met with an executive group about an upcoming management retreat. They had hired me to lead and facilitate the retreat and we met to do a preliminary analysis of their needs. When asked about their biggest challenge they unanimously replied that their management team needed to plan more proactively and needed to run each department like its own company within the company. The executive team was tired of having managers come to them frequently for solutions and wanted to create an environment where the managers came up with solutions on their own.

When I asked what they had done so far to create this change the room got very quiet. The executives knew what they wanted but they hadn't thought about how to create it or communicate it so that the situation would indeed change.

Empowerment is an overdone buzzword but a much-wanted skill within an organization. But it is a double-edged sword: constant change and communication is required to ensure that empowerment doesn't turn into mass chaos.

Action

- Create a self-sufficient mindset within your team.

    Be clear on what decisions you want people to make on their own and what decisions require checking in with upper management.

    Write down the process for handling common issues and provide guidelines for decision-making.

    Give people the freedom to do what you want them to do. Don't punish them if they make a decision that wasn't the best. Instead use it as a training opportunity.

- Encourage managers to align their teams' goals with one or more main goals of the organization as a whole. Ensure they know how to keep the overall goal in mind when making decisions. For instance, a good question might be, "Will this decision benefit the company and its profitability overall?"

- Pat them on the back when they make their own decisions or find their own solutions. Reward them publicly and encourage them to continue the behaviour.

Why You'll Love It

When you set guidelines for decision-making and proactive planning you have provided a process to follow. This frees you up for other duties. You can allow your team to do what needs to be done while knowing they are all working with an overall plan.

Why They'll Love It

Having the freedom to make decisions within clear parameters allows the team to plan for the future and to take personal responsibility for adhering to the plan.

Open Your Door— But Not All the Time

Open and accessible leadership has been touted as the ideal. It is true that leaders need to be easy to approach, accessible and trustworthy. However, when you want to create an autonomous and independent team it is sometimes useful not to be accessible.

A leader I worked with had a fantastic way of handling this so that she maintained an aura of accessibility and still set boundaries. She put a plastic file folder holder on the wall right outside her office, to be used when her door was shut. The note on it was set in large type.

If you need an answer you have three choices:

1. Write it down and I will get back to you by the end of the day.
2. Find someone else who can answer your question.
3. Look it up; do research for your answer.

This forces others to think before they approach her with repeated or silly questions. Another gentleman uses yellow "Keep Out" tape and puts it across his doorway when he cannot be interrupted. These are unique ways of letting others know when you are available and what to do when you are not.

We as leaders can be guilty of training our direct reports to become too reliant on us. We need to change the rules so our team has to use its own resources and become more independent. Just remember, use the appearance of inaccessibility carefully. If you use it all of the time then you really *are* being inaccessible!

Action

- Come up with a creative and humorous way of handling interruptions or creating boundaries so that you can make better use of your time.
- Think of ways you and your team could create quiet times or specific time-blocks for uninterrupted work. Teams who have done this have found that their productivity went up dramatically.

Why You'll Love It

Interruptions and constant open-door visits can become intrusive and waste time. You gain time and energy if you set boundaries. You may also notice that your team does not come to you as often for small things.

Why They'll Love It

Communicated expectations make everybody happy. As long as the team knows when you are available and what to do when you are not, they'll feel prepared to handle it.

Avoid the Favourites Trap

Lead the life that will make you kindly and friendly to everyone about you, and you will be surprised what a happy life you will lead.

Charles M Schwab

As leaders we all have our favourite employees on the team. We may like them as people, or they might have a similar work style to ours. There are dangers to playing favourites and we need to remind ourselves now and again to be careful not to fall into the favourites trap.

The dangers of playing favourites are:

- The favourite begins to feel superior to the rest of the team because of his or her alliance with the leader.
- The rest of the team stops trying hard because they feel

that the favourite gets all of the attention.
- Those with lower self-esteem may resort to poor performance to get attention.
- The favourite gets burned out.
- The favourite may divulge information that you have only shared with him or her, which in turn undermines your leadership.

Think about this specifically as it applies to delegation. It is easier to delegate to the same people because we know what we can expect. This can work against us: those to whom we over-delegate become burdened with a greater workload and the rest of the team gets away with doing less.

When delegating to people who haven't done a lot for you in the past, notice that they may try to get out of the task because they lack confidence. The best way to begin delegation in that case is to offer guidance and assistance, and to re-affirm your faith in their abilities to get it done and done right. Also, you will want to communicate your desire to share the workload equally within the team.

Action
- Have a meeting with your team and talk about shared delegation.

- Put all tasks and projects up on a board or flip chart and ask that each of them pick two of the tasks. The rules are that everyone has to take two and no one can take more.
- If you find yourself continually delegating to the same person, force yourself to re-think this. Who would benefit most from the delegated task? How could you give them the resources to be able to do the job at a high level?

Why You'll Love It

From a leadership perspective the more shared delegation there is, the more you can relax when you are away from the office for short or long periods of time.

Why They'll Love It

A fair leader is respected far more than a leader who plays favourites. The team feels more like a team.

One Bad Apple
Spoils the Barrel

We are not just managing for the sake of being great managers.
We are managing for the mission.

Frances Hesselbein

Leaders can become attached or feel obligated to certain individuals because they complete a lot of work or simply because they will do anything the leader asks. But if that individual is sabotaging the team's overall goals, his or her attitude can poison the entire work atmosphere.

One client of mine had a sales team of six. The top performer had been with the company for a while, knew the business inside and out, and produced large sales. But he didn't get along with his teammates and he treated less-desirable suppliers or clients with disdain and disrespect. The owner of the company was afraid to deal with this employee because he felt that his business would suffer. In fact the employee was holding the entire company hostage and everyone knew it. Finally the havoc being wreaked grew to be so unbearable that the owner, after agonizing over what to do and having meeting after meeting about the employee's less-than-desirable interpersonal skills, finally let him go.

As soon as the situation was dealt with the owner's fears turned out to be unfounded. The rest of the team performed more efficiently. It is amazing how one person can make such a huge and powerful impression on a group, whether positive or negative.

I am not saying that if someone doesn't fit or isn't cutting it that they should immediately be fired. In fact, I advocate doing whatever we can to support that person with coaching and ongoing dialogue. Still, eventually we need ask ourselves—and the employee—if we are trying to fit a square peg into a round hole. The best leaders are those who coach their people to their highest level of happiness, which may end up being somewhere else.

Action

- Ask yourself who in your team could improve his or her

attitude, teamwork, or customer-care skills.

- Coach these people consistently on the new behaviours you need from them.
- Begin the discipline process by having face-to-face meetings and documenting them.
- Ask yourself the following questions:

  Am I afraid to deal with this person because of his or her performance or previous contributions?

  Am I willing to let the behaviour continue and negatively affect the rest of the team?

  When am I going to deal with (issue/name)?

Why You'll Love It

You will have less daily stress!

Why They'll Love It

Your team will sigh with relief, perform at higher levels and be more positive.

Get the X Factor

Our spirits grow grey before our hairs.

Charles Lamb

John F Kennedy had it, Bill Clinton has it, and Nelson Mandela has it. What is it? It is the X factor.

Do you believe great leaders are born, not made? Like any inherent gift, leadership is easier for some than for others, but leadership is a learned skill. With lifelong learning the X factor can be developed for any leader.

The X factor consists of the following traits:

- Open-mindedness
- Broad perspectives
- Ability to laugh at oneself
- Charisma and contagious energy
- Sense of humour
- Ability to connect with a variety of personalities

- Focus
- Organization
- Orientation to detail
- Thoroughness
- Time consciousness
- Project orientation
- Clear communication
- Fairness

Think of a leader you know and admire, someone you may have worked for or with. This person will display a number of these qualities, if not all of them. Superb leaders are balanced in their strengths and gather people around them who support their weaker areas.

Action

- Rate yourself on a scale of one to ten with ten being high on each of the above traits.
- Where are your strengths?
- Which traits could you further develop or improve?
- What course could you take or what book could you read to help you do better in the areas you need to improve?
- When are you going to take action?

Why You'll Love It

Balanced skill sets increase your confidence and your abilities.

Why They'll Love It

All personality styles will appreciate your well-rounded abilities and respect your contributions.

The Truth? They Can Handle It

If you don't stand for something, you'll fall for anything.

Steve Bartkowski

Many corporate leaders feel that too much information can be a dangerous thing, so they avoid sharing the whole truth or communicating all aspects of an event or change to the rest of the company. When I ask why, they often say things like, "They don't need to know," or "They might overreact" or "It'll only complicate matters." But when I interview managers and employees and ask them how work is going, they inevitably mention the possibility of the very thing the executive did not want to discuss! In most cases people already know; or worse, they are adding speculation and gossip, inflating the problem even further.

Employees I have surveyed said the top two things they want from their executives are openness and truth. In other words, if you know that people are going to be laid off but continue to deny it people will lower their productivity naturally out of fear, anger, or worse, apathy. However, if the CEO openly admits that layoffs are likely, he or she can also use the opportunity to discuss possible benefits the re-structuring may provide, such as new jobs and re-training, and support for career changes, just to name a few.

He or she could reassure and calm others by saying (and meaning) the following: "I will personally work to ensure that we will do our utmost to protect as many jobs as possible, and for those who will not have jobs, prepare you for the outside workplace." At this point the leader has given people an opportunity to make personal choices about what they want to do.

Action

- Admit to your team or group when you are afraid, worried, or unsure. You will not lose respect. You will gain it, because they will see that you are human and have the same concerns they do.

- Then state what can be done and what your commitment is to the solution. Your team is looking to its leader to show courage.

Why You'll Love It

It's just plain easier to tell the truth. You don't have to remember the untruths, and you have less stress.

Why They'll Love It

Employees feel safer and perform better in a work environment that is open and honest.

What's Your Story?

Dreaming illustrates your hidden capacities and your unawakened ability.

Peter Daniels

Dynamic leaders have stories, legends and myths told about them. Stories inspire people; they bypass the logical brain and expand how others see you. Stories humanize you. Myth or fact, your stories can help shape the work environment and create a space for sharing in a non-linear fashion.

Every hero or heroine has a story. For example, Donald Trump's story starts with working for his father, buying his first building in New York, losing all his money, and rising again.

We love stories about those who came from nothing and turned into something because it shows us that humble beginnings can still make a hero.

In the book *The Traveler's Gift* (Thomas Nelson, 2002)

the story is of a man at the height of his career who took a fall. His journey back to greater success began with the wisdom of men from history. Robin Sharma's book, *The Monk Who Sold His Ferrari* (HarperCollins Canada, 1999), became a bestseller because of the lessons revealed within the story.

So what's your story? What's your background? What do you strive for?

Action

- Keep a journal to write down stories about you, your family and your work.
- Travel with the journal: take it in your car, on the train, on the plane—gather your thoughts there.
- Share your goals and visions with others through stories.

Why You'll Love It

It is creative and fun to think in stories. You will find your creativity expands and your enjoyment increases.

Why They'll Love It

Everyone loves a good story! When your team hears your history and your direction in stories it is memorable and meaningful.

Don't "Should" All Over

44

Honest criticism is hard to take, particularly from a relative, a friend, an acquaintance, or a stranger.

Franklin P Jones

Whenever we "should" all over someone they don't like it. Whenever we "should" all over ourselves it doesn't feel good.

"Should" is a word that focuses on the past and the problem and does not move us forward. Strong leaders are careful communicators, or as I call them in my book *Say What You Mean, Mean What You Say,* conscious communicators.

Words are powerful. Leaders who focus their communication on the future and on finding solutions will find themselves motivating others at very high levels.

When we tell people they should or shouldn't do

something we are pushing our opinions on to them. Their automatic response is to become defensive and push back. Think about this. Most of us have an automatic response to being told we should do something, such as: "Says who?"

Instead, replace the word "should" with "next time" to keep the other person focused on the future and what they can do, rather than focusing on what is already done and cannot be changed. You can also apply this principle to yourself—many of us say things like "I should have known better" or "I shouldn't have done it that way."

Although learning from our mistakes is a good thing, dumping all over ourselves doesn't do anything for us other than slow us down and make us feel bad about ourselves. Instead of "should-ing" on yourself or others, focus on what you have control over—your actions for the future.

Action

- Next time you find yourself being hard on yourself or second-guessing something you did, analyze the situation this way:

    What did I like best about how I behaved, led or communicated?

    What would I like to improve for the next time?

- Use these same questions when coaching others to help them focus on the future and solutions.

Why You'll Love It

You will feel less guilty and less like a martyr. Take action, not the blame.

Why They'll Love It

Focusing forward creates more energy and gives people something positive to do.

Encourage Gossip

Yup, you heard right. Gossip can be a good thing. Positive gossip is a very good thing.

Gossip, although annoying, is never going to go away in any environment where people gather. It's human nature and most people think it's fun. But negative gossip can be destructive to a team's performance or to a company's morale.

A few companies have taken a different approach to the gossip challenge. They held staff meetings where they addressed the challenges of gossip, then introduced a new policy called "Positive Gossip Only". They put up large posters saying "We Practice Positive Gossip Here" with pictures of people talking, laughing and smiling. The idea was that if people were going to gossip, they were encouraged to do it in a positive way.

As leaders we need to uphold this ideal even more than our employees do. I used to be one of the worst culprits until I was promoted to leadership and realized that gossip was going to hurt me as I moved ahead. The next time you find yourself in the midst of negative gossip, try shifting the gossip from negative to positive.

Action

- The next time someone gossips, ask the gossiper:
  Have you said this directly to the person involved?
  Would this person be okay with you telling me this?
  Is this going to help this person, hurt this person, or teach him or her a lesson?
- Encourage positive gossip, which focuses on impressive or positive things that others are doing.

Why You'll Love It

When you get in the habit of focusing on how to gossip positively it becomes easier to focus on what's right with someone versus what's wrong. You'll feel better about yourself.

Why They'll Love It

Positive gossip boosts morale and peer support.

You Are Perfect— Perfectly Human

My philosophy is that not only are you responsible for your life, but doing the best at this moment puts you in the best place for the next moment.

Oprah Winfrey

Some people assume that just because we are in leadership positions that we are perfect. Well, we are—we are perfectly human.

Good leaders are not afraid to show their fears and feelings. Instead of feeling vulnerable they have strong self-esteem around their talents and abilities. Solid leaders never forget the deeply personal element of being a leader and how important it is to speak to personal issues when appropriate.

Recently I worked with an executive who was going

through a tough time in her personal life. She had suddenly become ill while travelling and was diagnosed with stomach cancer. It was shocking and stressful for her and she needed to take short-term disability while she went through chemotherapy and other treatments. Her team back at the office was of course concerned and upset. But in her effort to get back to "business as usual" she did not address the cancer with anyone, thus creating an uncomfortable environment for her employees.

When we began working together I encouraged her to meet one-on-one with each of her team members to let them know how the cancer affected her and that she wanted them to feel comfortable with her as they moved forward.

This same leader held a team meeting after she had spoken to her team members individually. She told everyone that she'd been through a tough ordeal and that it scared her. She went on to tell them how it re-affirmed her commitment to them and their goals. This built deeper connections with her team and increased their commitment to working together.

Action

- Think of ways that you can share a little more of your personal side with your team. Remember that this is a balancing act, because over-sharing can create other problems.

Why You'll Love It

Showing your personal fears and concerns allows you to be authentic as a leader. You will find you can address non-personal hidden or secret issues more easily as well.

Why They'll Love It

Authenticity demonstrated by a leader builds trust and loyalty.

Create
and Innovate

Creativity involves taking what you have, where you are, and getting the most out of it.

Carl Mays

Creative problem-solving is a teachable skill. The saying "think outside the box" has become an overused cliché, but putting the concept into action is relevant in today's business climate.

An article in the August 2003 issue of *Scientific American* characterized the '90s as the decade of the brain and the first decade of the 2000s as the decade of behaviour. I interpret that to mean that it no longer matters as much how much we know, it's what we are *doing* with what we know that matters the most. Intellectual knowledge is only as important as how it is used for business and personal growth, and innovation.

The more creative thinking we can inspire as leaders, the more the people on our teams will begin to see problem-solving as an enjoyable challenge rather than something to be dreaded. Often in seminars I will lead a creative group exercise in which participants have to come up with a dozen things that a cat and a refrigerator have in common. At first everyone gives me weird looks but after they get started I hear lots of laughs and aha's as they realize how many commonalities there really are.

Then I announce that there are over fifty possible answers to that creative problem-solving exercise. They are shocked.

Creative thinking activities as an ongoing team exercise can bring energy, ideas, and fun to meetings and to daily problem-solving.

Action

- At your next meeting teach your team how to mind-map. A mind map is simply a circle drawn in the middle of a blank piece of paper with a problem, idea or starting concept listed in the circle. Any idea remotely linked to that central idea is quickly written down as another linked circle. Keep going until the page is full. Do not censor or edit the ideas as they flow. Once done, look at the whole page and see what pops out—chances are that the possible solution is there somewhere.

- Read the book *How to Think Like Leonardo DaVinci* by Michael Gelb (Dell, 2000).

Why You'll Love It

Expanding your creative abilities leads to greater job satisfaction and confidence.

Why They'll Love It

Employees surveyed by the American Management Association listed creativity as one of the top ten things they look for in a satisfying work environment.

Take a Hero's Journey

Leaders know that the higher up you go—the more gently down your reach.

Sheila Murray Bethel

Leadership is a journey, a search for excellence and greater understanding of self. The rewards come when we relinquish the need to speak with authority and instead listen to what others have to contribute. There will always be someone who is wiser, so when we speak with thoughtfulness and presence our leadership shines through effortlessly.

Don't expect instant credibility. Instead recognize the need to earn credibility and respect. Being made a leader does not imply superiority and the right to autocracy. Being a leader gives us the opportunity to guide, support and sometimes humbly defer to the wisdom of others.

The journey cannot be taken alone. We cannot run ahead of the others to prove we know where we are going. We need to look ahead while staying with the group to encourage, cheer, and work towards combined success.

Internal growth during the leadership journey will be phenomenal if we acknowledge the learning process. We know we have successfully made the hero's journey when we recognize that our success was not self-created, but instead was "all-of-us-created". We lead best when we focus on our team, its needs and its goals.

Action

- Take some time to think about how members of your team could provide guidance, direction and goals for the team as a whole.
- Acknowledge yourself as a hero. Accept with graciousness the leadership and direction you have given to others. Make it symbolic—buy yourself something that symbolizes heroism and inspires you, such as a picture of your favourite leader.

Why You'll Love It

What you have learned on your hero's journey is expressed in other facets of your leadership. Learn and grow.

Why They'll Love It

Your team will feel a greater connection to you when you share what you've learned on your journey. They will have a stronger willingness to work hard when you lead as part of the team.

Listen and
Let Them Solve It

There was a definite process by which one made people into friends, and it involved talking to them and listening to them for hours at a time.

Rebecca West

Superb leaders have mastered the art of listening. Good listening skills are clear indicators of leadership excellence. Leaders who listen well have learned that instead of immediately trying to solve others' problems they need to listen carefully, reflect the message back and allow the other person to communicate a solution.

When I worked with my first coach over a dozen years ago he told me I was a lousy listener. He said the three rules of listening are as follows.

> 1. Shut up
> 2. Pay attention
> 3. Let them finish!

The rules may sound harsh but I have never forgotten them. Most of us only half-listen. We presume we know what the other person is saying or going to say. Usually when a conversation is happening both parties are listening and also thinking about what they are going to say next. This means there are typically three conversations going on: me with myself, me with you and you with yourself. All this while the two of us are trying to have a conversation!

We use reflective listening while the other person is talking—we do not say a word except to show we are listening and to encourage the other person to continue. We turn off the voice in our head that might be saying, "Steak for dinner, yeah, that'd be nice…" and we don't think about what we are going to say next. Instead we focus completely on the other

person. Once the person has finished we reflect back or para-
phrase what we heard and then move to either a solution or
continued dialogue. Listening in this way helps others to see
their own solutions more quickly. It also helps us not to automatically give the answer, which can allow others to become
overly dependent on us. In action it might look like this:

Jane: I am so upset at Joe for the way he spoke to me at
the meeting. I am so frustrated. Why do I even bother
to work hard when he makes comments like that?

Listener: Go on.

Jane: I am so angry I just want to walk over there and
give him the what-for.

Listener: I can understand why you are frustrated. What
are you going to do?

Jane: Well, uh... I thought you could help.

Listener: From what I heard you say, you think talking to
Joe might be the answer.

Jane: Yes, but I guess I need to calm down first.

Listener: That's a great idea. What are you going to do to
help you calm down?

Listening in a reflective way is powerful in any situation,
and can save much time in the long run because people are

given the space to feel heard and then can come up with their own solutions.

Action

- Answer the following questions:

    How often do you plan your response while the other person is speaking?

    How often do you judge the value of the speaker's message based on appearance and delivery?

    How often do you listen without eliminating external and internal distractions?

    How often do you interrupt?

    How often do you jump to conclusions before the speaker is finished?

    How often do you talk more than listen?

    How often do you forget to show the speaker you are listening with appropriate words or gestures?

    How often do you neglect to listen for feelings as well as for facts?

    How often do you fail to summarize the conversation to confirm your understanding?

- The more you answered "often" the more attention you need to pay to the art of listening.

Why You'll Love It

The better listener you are the less you need to jump in and fix things. You'll begin to feel less like a glorified babysitter and more like a sounding board for others' creative problem-solving.

Why They'll Love It

When people feel heard they will find solutions quicker than if others feed it to them or do it for them. Their confidence goes up and so does their ability to problem-solve.

Leader, Take Care of Thyself

> This above all: to thine own self be true; And it must follow, as the night the day; Thou canst not then be false to any man.
>
> *William Shakespeare,* Hamlet, Act I, Scene iii

We started this book with you and so we end it. As a leader it is all about you and has nothing to do with you, if you know what I mean.

Notice your personal performance abilities and your cycles of output. Stress can absolutely cripple us if we do not notice our stressors and triggers and proactively take care of ourselves with healthy outlets. Letting off steam is crucial to maintaining high performance levels and being able to lead without burning out.

Negative responses due to stress may be caused by:

- seeing limited alternatives
- fear of failure
- frequent complaints
- abandoning projects shortly after beginning them
- coming up with perfectly good reasons not to change
- thinking that we are trapped or have limited power.

Action

- Things that we can do to stay excited, invigorated and energetic are:

> See everything as a learning opportunity
> See conflict and people problems as challenges
> Grow through the experiences of working with others
> Maintain non-work-related hobbies or interests
> EXERCISE
> Eat right
> Get support from family and friends
> Seek support in the form of self-care, such as massage, vacations and time off.

Practically every human endeavour requires leadership. Zig Ziglar says, "Even a tow-car parade gets fouled up if you don't decide ahead of time who's going to lead." Leadership can be rewarding, engaging and fun when we embrace the responsibility. Continue leading at high levels, work to leave a legacy, and make a positive difference with the people you lead. God bless.

Order online at:
www.trafford.com/robots/03-1297.html

ISBN 141200928-6